Alphabet for American Children Coloring Book

Patrick Torma

authorHOUSE®

AuthorHouse™
1663 Liberty Drive
Bloomington, IN 47403
www.authorhouse.com
Phone: 1-800-839-8640

First published by AuthorHouse 7/1/2010

ISBN: 978-1-4520-5232-8 (e)
ISBN: 978-1-4520-5231-1 (sc)

Printed in the United States of America
Bloomington, Indiana

This book is printed on acid-free paper.

About Patrick the Patriot

Patrick is a 12 year old honor roll student in the 7th grade. His mom joined a group called As A Mom (http://asamom.org) and they inspired this creation. Patrick's mom was in the chat room when one of the other mommies said her daughter was singing C is for cookie. The chat decided that there was a need for a Patriot Alphabet to teach children. Patrick and his mom decided to create this project.

All the illustrations in this book were drawn by Patrick. He donated a major part of his Spring Break 2010 vacation to working on these drawings.

Patrick is inspired by the Tea Party movement and has attended several of their events. He enjoys Fox News and in particular Glenn Beck's show.

His hobbies include reading, drawing, playing his guitar, and of course, video games. He recently placed second in the Regional Science Fair in Arlington, VA.

America - The United States of America

A is for

<u>A</u>dams – John Adams was the 2nd President and one of our country's leading Founding Fathers. He was the key reason Congress accepted the Declaration of Independence.

Abraham Lincoln – Our 16th President who led his country through its greatest internal crisis, the American Civil War, preserving the Union and ending slavery.

B is for

Blessings – Count your Blessings every day.

B is for

Ben Franklin – Another of our Founding Fathers. He also helped create the Constitution.

B is for

Brave – America is the Land of the Free and Home of the Brave.

C is for

<u>C</u>onstitution – The Constitution of the United States is a special
document. Read it.

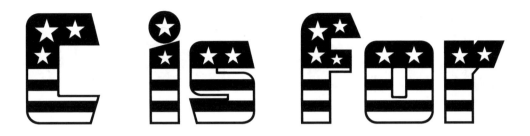

C is for

Colonies – There were 13 original Colonies in America.

New York

New Hampshire

Maine

Massachusetts

Pennsylvania

Connecticut

New Jersey

Maryland

Rhode island

Delaware

Virginia

Atlantic Ocean

North Carolina

Georgia

South Carolina

PT

C is For

Crocket – Davy Crocket was a Congressman who died defending the Alamo.

D is for

<u>D</u>eclaration of Independence– The document that freed America on July 4, 1776.

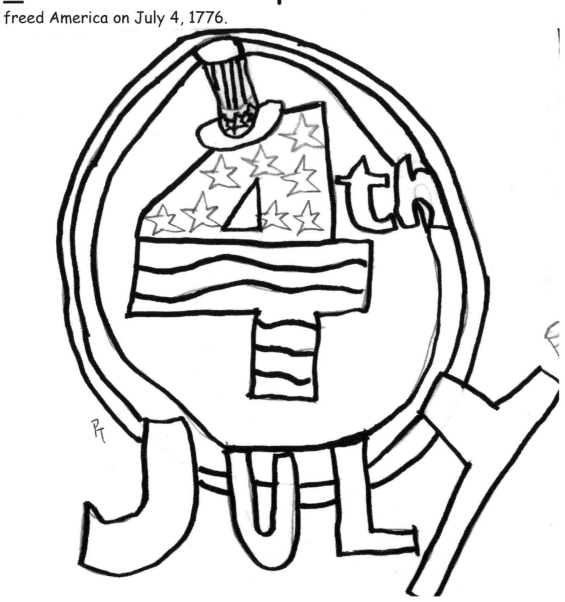

D is for

Daniel Boone – Daniel Boone was a famous American pioneer.

D is for

D-Day- June 6, 1944 - The Battle of Normandy in WWII

<u>E</u>agle – The American Bald Eagle is a symbol of our country.

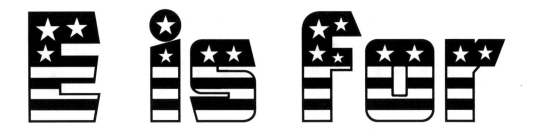

E is for

Education – Learn your American History.

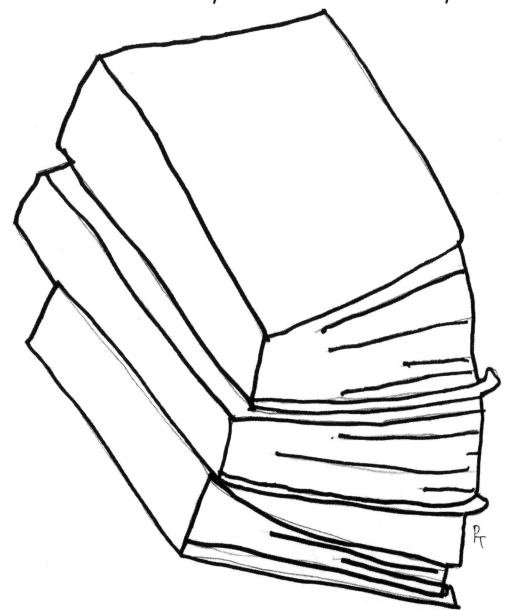

Effort – It took great effort to make and keep America free.

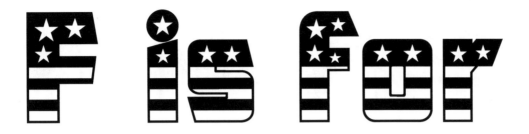

F is for

Founding Fathers – The key founding fathers: <u>Benjamin Franklin</u>, <u>George Washington</u>, <u>John Adams</u>, <u>Thomas Jefferson</u>, <u>John Jay</u>, <u>James Madison</u>, and <u>Alexander Hamilton</u>.

F is for

Freedom – "The right of freedom being a gift from God, it is not in the power of man to alienate this gift and voluntarily become a slave." ~Samuel Adams

Can you find your way through the maze to Freedom?

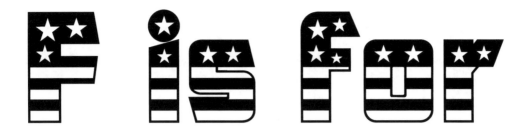

F is for

<u>F</u>lag– The American flag is the symbol of our nation's strength and unity.

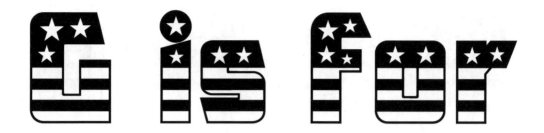

G is for

God– God Bless America. Faith in God was important to our Founding Fathers.

G is For

George Washington – Our 1st President and the general who led the winning of the American Revolution.

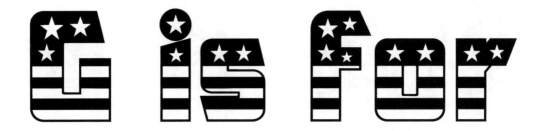

<u>G</u>lory– Glory is great praise and honor. Our flag is referred to as Old Glory.

Honor– Honor your Parents. Honor your Elders and Honor your Country.

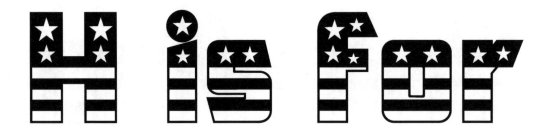

H is for

<u>H</u>istory– History repeats itself if it is not learned.

Proud to Be An AMERICAN

H is for

Hamilton– Alexander Hamilton was one of the Founding Fathers.

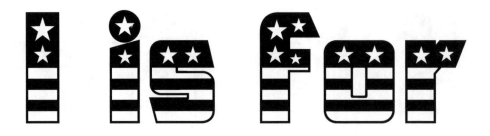

Independence– Independence is the self governing of a nation.

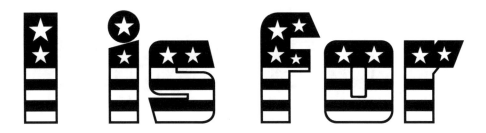

Ingenuity— Is the skill of cleverness in devising. Our Founding Fathers had ingenuity in designing the Constitution.

Unscramble the Words

1. _ _ _ _ _
   A V B E R

2. _ _ _ _ _
   O O N H R

3. _ _ _ _ _ _ _ _
   C S F A I I R E C

4. _ _ _ _ _ _ _
   L E S N I E C

5. _ _ _ _ _ _ _ _ _ _ _
   S I M C E A T I R   A D Y

6. _ _ _ _ _
   Y P O P P

7. _ _ _ _ _
   E P C A E

8. _ _ _ _ _ _ _
   E E T V A N R

9. _ _ _ _ _ _
   F D N E E D

10. _ _ _ _ _ _ _ _
    M M E B E E R R

➢ Hints
1. Courageous
2. To treat with respect
3. To suffer loss for a cause
4. The absence of sound
5. Veteran's Day (original name)
6. Symbolic flower
7. Calm and quiet. Not at war
8. A person who has served in the military
9. To guard, protect or shield from danger
10. Recall. Bring to mind

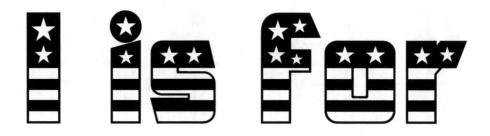

I Love America – Love your Country.

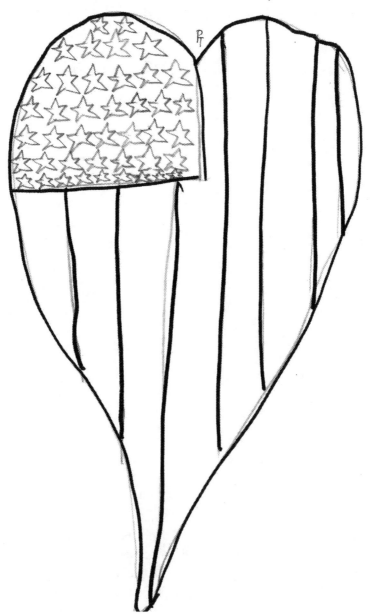

J is for

<u>J</u>ustice – Liberty and Justice for all.

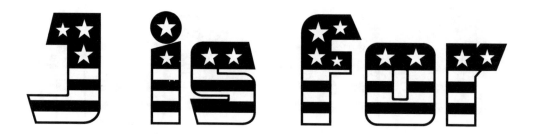

Jefferson – Thomas Jefferson was the 3rd President, the main author of the Declaration of Independence and a Founding Father.

Jackson– Andrew Jackson was the 7th President of the US. He was first president primarily associated with the American Frontier.

K is for

Knowledge – "Knowledge is of no value unless you put it into practice."
~ Andrew Chekhov

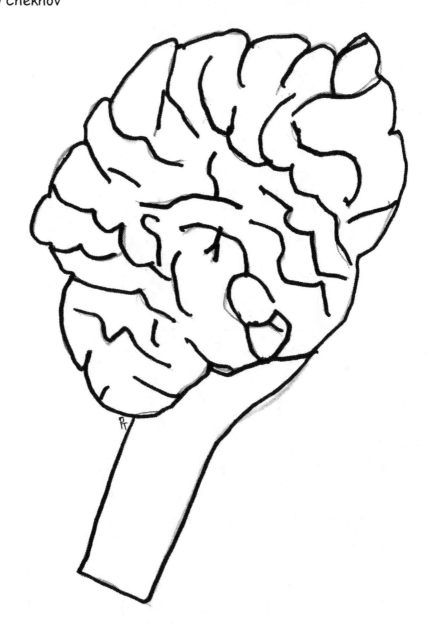

King – Kings do not exist in the United States. The American Revolution refused having a king.

K is for

<u>Ke</u>y –   The Key to keeping our Freedom is to read the Constitution and obey it.

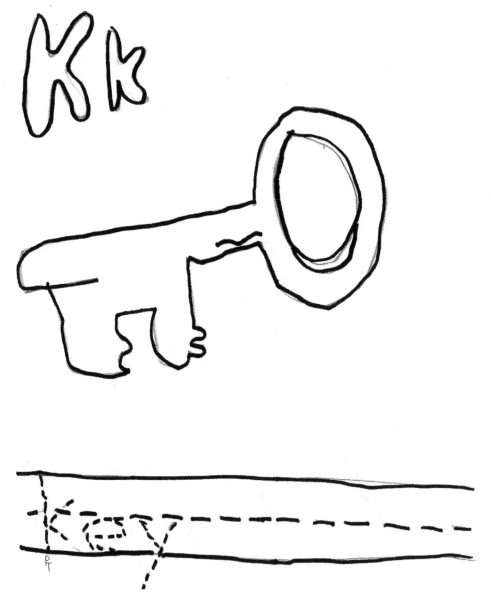

<u>L</u>aw – "A government of LAWS, not men." ~ John Adams

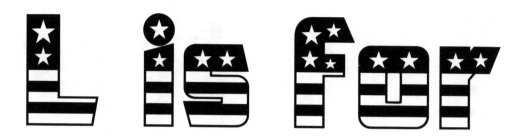

Love – Love and Honor your Country and your Parents.

Liberty – Means that individual has the right to act according to his or her own will.

<u>M</u>om – A mother is one to whom you hurry when you are troubled. ~ Emily Dickinson

HELP the kid get the flower to the Mother

M is for

Madison – James Madison was the 4th President and a Founding Father. He was known as the "Father of the Constitution".

M is for

<u>M</u>ilitary – Those who volunteer to fight for our freedom.

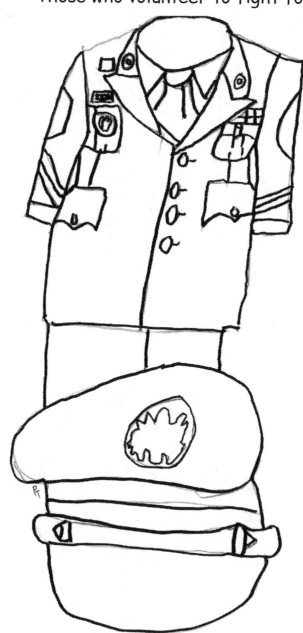

Nation – One Nation Under God

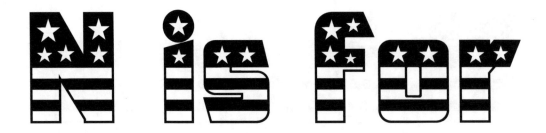

N is for

<u>N</u>eighbor – Love thy Neighbor.

Nice – To be nice is to be pleasing or agreeable in nature.

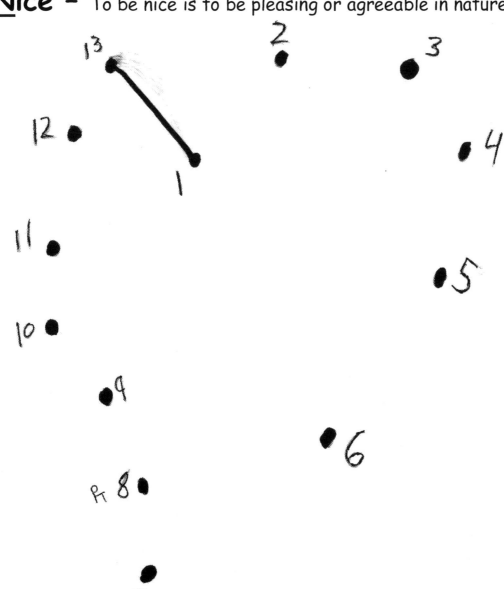

Opportunity – America offers the best opportunities in the world.

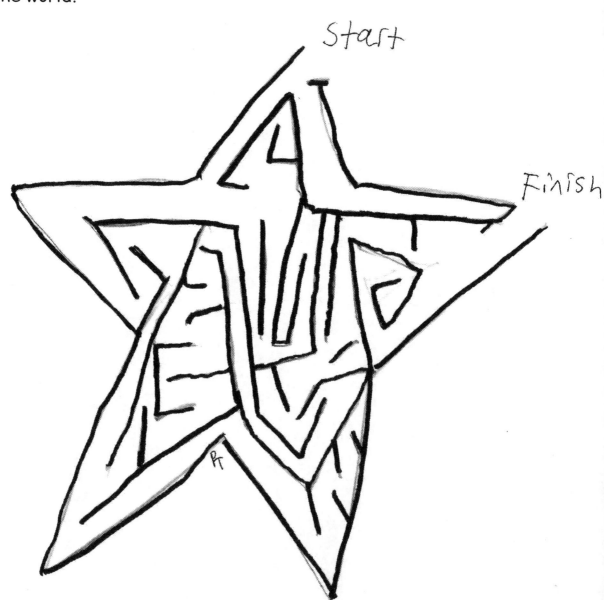

 O is for

Oppose – Oppose losing your Freedom and your American Rights.

O is for

<u>**O**</u>**pen** – Open your mind to learning your American Rights.

P is for

Patriot – A Patriot is one who loves and defends his or her country.

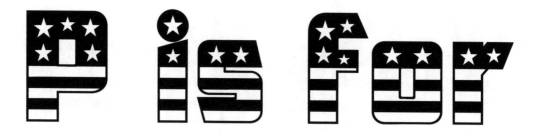

P is for

Prosperity — Prosperity is the condition of being successful or thriving.

Purpose –

Purpose is a result, end, aim, or goal of an action intentionally taken.

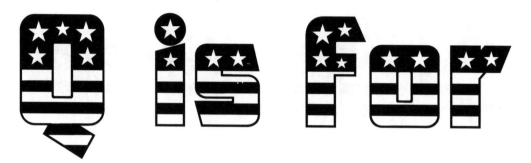

Q is for

Quest – A quest is an exploration. Your quest is to read and save the Constitution.

Start ★

Finish

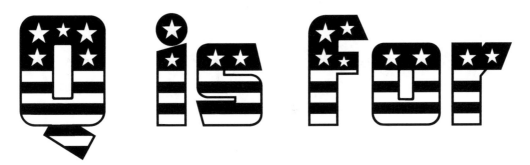 **Q is for**

Question – "Question with Boldness" ~ Thomas Jefferson

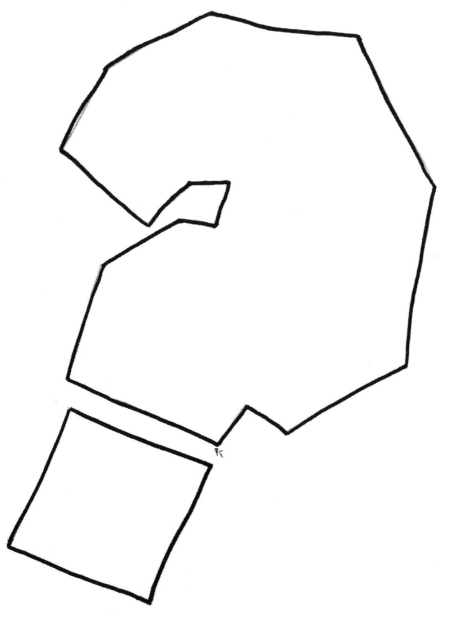

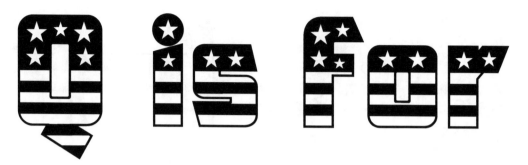

Quit – "Quit taxing us to death". ~ Eric Y

The Boston Tea Party

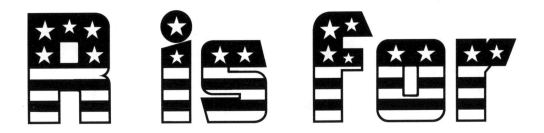

Republic – A Republic is a form of government in which the citizens choose their leaders.

R is for

<u>R</u>ights – "We hold these truths to be self-evident, that all men are created equal, that they are endowed by their Creator with certain *unalienable Rights*".

Bill of Rights
I have the right to....

R is for

<u>R</u>espect — Respect is the condition of being honored.

S is For

Stars & **S**tripes – The national flag of the United States of America.

Stars

Stripes

S is For

Samuel Adams – Samuel Adams was another Founding Father of the United States. He was John Adams' second cousin.

S is for

State's Rights – State's Rights are guaranteed in the 10th Amendment of the Constitution.

T is for

Truth – "You can bend it and twist it... You can misuse and abuse it... But even God cannot change the Truth." ~ Michael Levy

Start

Finish

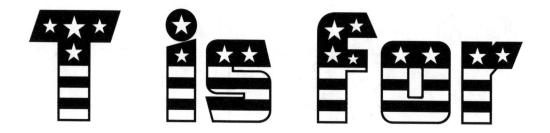

<u>T</u>homas Paine – Thomas Paine was an author, inventor, intellectual and one of the Founding Fathers of the United States.

T is for

Trust – "Faith is not belief without proof, but trust without reservation." ~ D. Elton Trueblood

U is for

U S A-

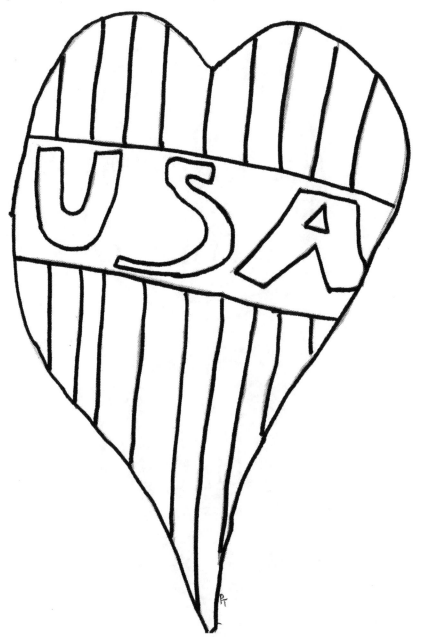

U is for

<u>U</u>nited – *"United we stand, divided we fall"*. ~ a motto

U is for

Ullyses S. Grant – The 18th President. He was a General in the Civil War and led the North to victory.

Value – "Values provide perspective in the best of times and the worst". ~ Charles Garfield

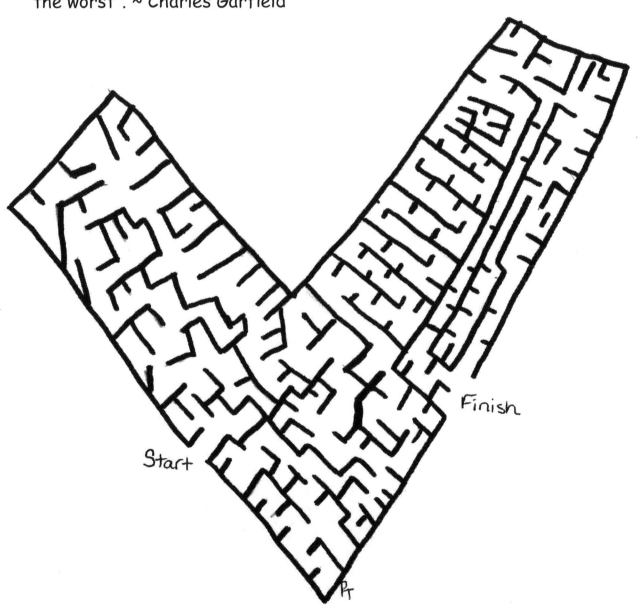

Start

Finish

V is for

Victory – "Victory at all costs, victory in spite of all terror, victory however long and hard the road may be; for without victory there is no survival." ~ Winston Churchill

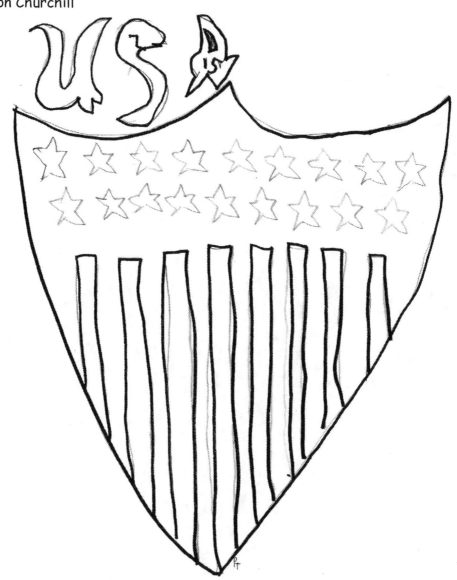

V is for

Vote – "Let each citizen remember at the moment he is offering his vote that he is not making a present or a compliment to please an individual - or at least that he ought not so to do; but that he is executing one of the most solemn trusts in human society for which he is accountable to God and his country." ~ Samuel Adams

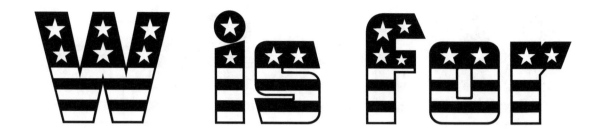

Washington D.C. — The Capitol of the United States.

W is for

Wisdom – "We are made wise not by the recollection of our past, but by the responsibility for our future". ~ George Bernard Shaw

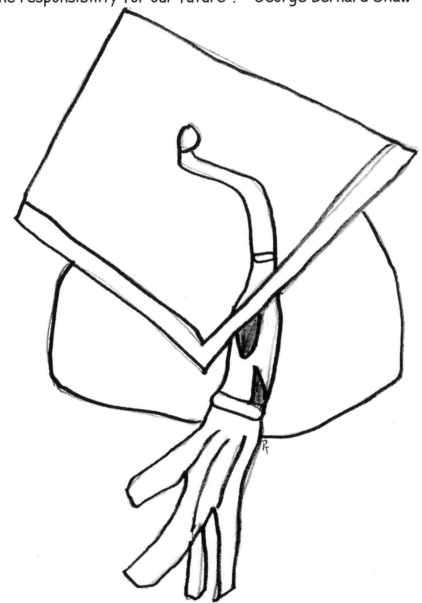

W is for

Write – "Let us tenderly and kindly cherish, therefore, the means of knowledge. Let us dare to read, think, speak, and write. Let us tenderly and kindly cherish, therefore, the means of knowledge. Let us dare to read, think, speak, and write." ~ John Adams

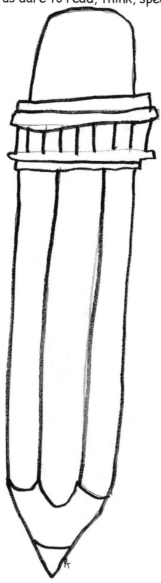

Xylophone – Learn to play the Star Spangled Banner on your xylophone.

X is for

<u>X</u>cited – Get e<u>X</u>cited about learning American History.

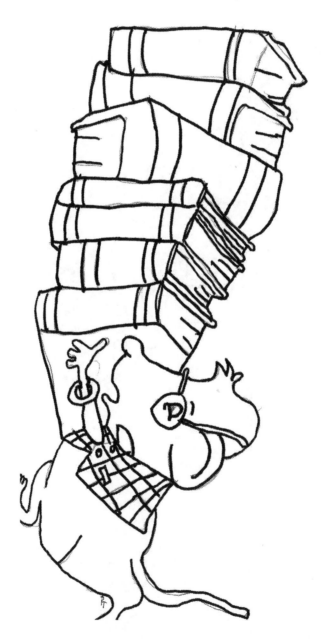

X is for

<u>X</u>cellence – Strive for e<u>X</u>cellence in everything you do.

Yankee Doodle – "Yankee Doodle went to town, a-riding on a pony; Stuck a feather in his cap and called it macaroni." ~ Richard Shuckburgh (Draw a feather in Yankee Doodle's hat.)

<u>Y</u>earn – "Can we doubt that only a Divine Providence placed this land, this island of freedom, here as a refuge for all those people in the world who yearn to breathe freely." ~ Ronald Reagan

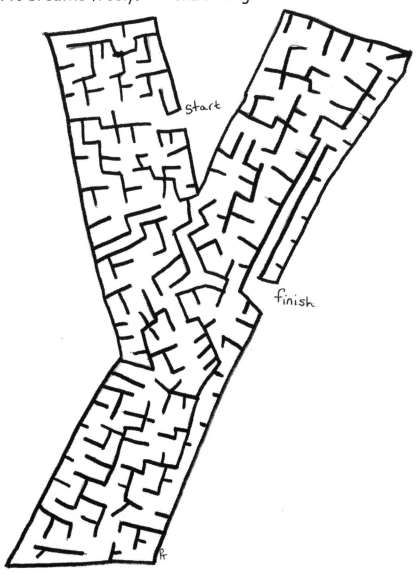

You– "I hope that when you're my age you'll be able to say, as I have been able to say: we lived in freedom, we lived lives that were a statement, not an apology." ~ Ronald Reagan

Draw a picture of your face in this box.

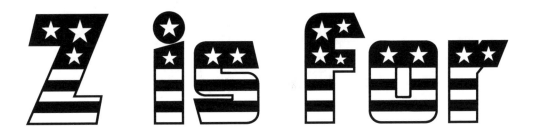

Z is for

<u>Z</u>ero – Have zero tolerance for losing your Constitutional rights.

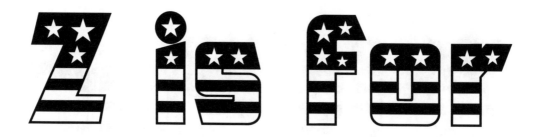

Z is For

Zeal– Zeal means to have an ardent interest in pursuing something.

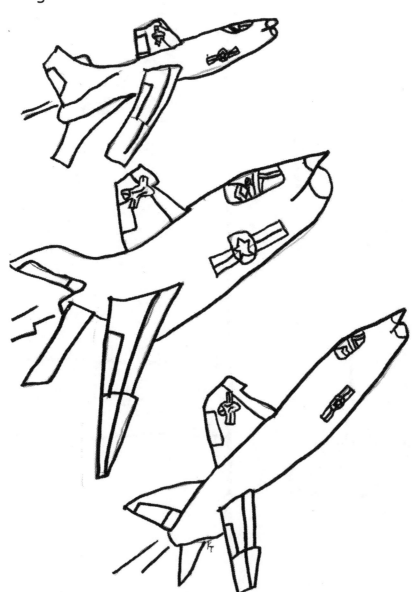

Z is for

Zest– Zest means a keen enjoyment. Always keep your zest for Freedom.

The Branches of the American Government

The Founding Fathers wrote the Constitution over 200 years ago. The Constitution is the wonderful document that tells the United States of America how our government should work. To be sure the government was not controlled by a king or just a small group of people, the Founding Fathers divided it into three parts. The Founding Fathers were afraid that one person or a small group of people could create a dictatorship or a tyrant. The three branches of government are:

1. The Executive Branch
2. The Legislative Branch
3. The Judicial Branch

The Branches of the American Government
The Legislative Branch

The Legislative branch of the government was created by Article I of the Constitution and makes the laws for the United States of America. It is headed by Congress but consists of government agencies such as the Library of Congress and the Government Printing Office. Congress has two parts, the House of Representatives and the Senate. There are 2 members in the Senate from every state. The number of Representatives for each state is determined by the population of that state. The Congress meets in the U.S. Capitol Building in Washington, D.C.

The Branches of the American Government
The Executive Branch

The Executive Branch was created by Article II, section 1 of the Constitution. The main duty of the Executive Branch is to make sure people follow the laws of the United States of America. The President is the head of the Executive Branch. His job is to carry out the federal laws. He is also the Commander and Chief which means he oversees the military and directs national defense. His other duties include dealing with international powers and foreign policy, performing ceremonial duties, and signing or vetoing laws presented to him from Congress. The Vice President and the Cabinet advise the President.

The Branches of the American Government
The Judicial Branch

The third branch of the government was created by Article III of the Constitution and is called the judicial branch. The judicial branch is made up of courts. The highest court in the United States of America is the U.S. Supreme Court. The U.S. Supreme Court is responsible for interpreting the Constitution and reviewing laws made by Congress.

"I pledge allegiance to the
Flag of the
United States of America,
and to the Republic for which it
stands,
one Nation under God,
indivisible,
with liberty and justice for all."